50 Things
I'm Going to Do before I Kill Myself

(and other tricks that keep me alive)

JAIME CAPENER

50 Things I'm Going to Do Before I Kill Myself
Copyright 2024 by Jaime Capener – All rights reserved, including the right to reproduce distribute, or transmit in any form or by any means.

Except as permitted under the U.S. Copyright Act of 1976, no part of this book may be reproduced, distributed, or transmitted in any form or by any means, or stored in a database or retrieval system without the written permission of the authors, except in the case of brief passages embodied in critical reviews and articles where the title, author and ISBN accompany such review or article.

For information contact: 50thingslist@gmail.com

Published by: Y Mountain Press

Book Design by Francine Eden Platt • Eden Graphics, Inc.

ISBN: 979-8-9899247-7-6

Library of Congress Number: pending

Manufactured in the United States of America

*This book is dedicated
to all those
who feel so broken
that they want to end their lives.*

A fragmented life
placed back together
piece by piece
with kindness,
love, and patience
until whole.

Now happy,
healthy,
grateful to the Soul
who sacrificed so much
for fragmented me.

– JAIME CAPENER

TABLE OF CONTENTS

Introduction 2

    CHAPTER ONE: **50 Things List** 4

    CHAPTER TWO: **What Would I Have Missed?** 8

    CHAPTER THREE: **Who Do You Want to Find You?** ... 10

    CHAPTER FOUR: **Bad Habit** 12

    CHAPTER FIVE: **Indecision Is Your Friend** 13

    CHAPTER SIX: **Go to a Funeral** 14

    CHAPTER SEVEN: **Death Is Inevitable (without Your Help)** 15

    CHAPTER EIGHT: **How Do You Know the Pain Will End after Killing Yourself?** 16

    CHAPTER NINE: **Don't You Love Your Friends, Family, and Kids?** 17

    CHAPTER TEN: **Find Something (*Anything*!) to Live For** 18

    CHAPTER ELEVEN: **Don't Believe the Lie** 20

    CHAPTER TWELVE: **Lifelines** 22

    CHAPTER THIRTEEN: **Be Rare. Be Unique. Be Weird** .. 24

Resources 26
Final Thoughts & Contact Info 27
Acknowledgments 28
Afterword 30
About the Author 35

INTRODUCTION

I was twelve years old, sitting on the stairs, listening to my mom and dad fight. My mom told my dad that one day she was downstairs in the office contemplating suicide when my big sister randomly came home for lunch, so she ran upstairs. Her attempt was thwarted.

I immediately started to cry. I ran downstairs into my bathroom, grabbed a razor blade, and held it to my wrist. "How could she leave us? Didn't she love us?"

My first attempt at suicide was a cry for help. A way of saying, "Am I not worth living for? If my mom doesn't love me enough to stick around, why am I sticking around?"

I survived my youth and didn't have any feelings of depression until I hit adulthood. I realized my reaction to stress was to remove myself entirely from the situation. My brain doesn't work like normal people's brain. Take my fear of heights, for example. When I get near an edge of a building or bridge or cliff, my brain says, "the fastest way out of this high place is to jump." Most people's brains would tell them to move back and go down the stairs. But my brain says, "to get yourself out of this stressful situation, take the path of least resistance: jump." I don't want to die when I'm standing up there, it's just my brain telling me that's the fastest way out.

This is the same experience I feel when I'm stressed, in pain, and depressed. I tend to think the fastest way out is to kill myself. In those moments I don't want to die. I want to live. The fight is to live. Death would be easy. Living is hard—living with the pain depression brings. In my opinion, every successful suicide happens because a person lost the fight to live.

This book is written to the person who is contemplating suicide. It may or may not use politically correct terms. When I was lying in bed and decided "today is the day," I honestly didn't care how my death would be described. The fact was, I was going to commit suicide. I was going to experience death by suicide. I was going to kill myself, yes, even commit murder on myself. The way that act was described after the fact didn't matter to me. I'm not writing to the professionals, the doctors, or the therapists. I'm writing this book to the person who has given up hope and feels so broken that they see no other way out, with no apologies.

The chapters of this book can stand alone and be read in any order. Not every chapter will connect with everyone. Find the chapter, sentence, or quote that resonates with you. Use this book in whatever way best serves you and your situation.

I'm not a doctor or psychologist. I'm a human being who has suffered and survived a deep and debilitating depression. These are the tips and tricks I came up with to help ME survive. If this book helps one person survive, it will be worth it.

I hope you are the ONE.

CHAPTER ONE

50 Things List

Once you're dead, you're dead. No more living. No more enjoying the sunsets. No more hearing laughter. No more feeling so cold your fingers and toes are numb. Before I die, I want to swallow, engulf, and experience all the mortal feels I can. So, I started a list and committed to accomplishing every item—50 things I'm going to do before I kill myself:

1. Swim with dolphins
2. Watch the sunset in Samoa
3. Go to the airport and get on a plane to anywhere
4. Kiss a stranger
5. Eat at ten Michelin star restaurants
6. Jump off the stratosphere in Las Vegas
7. Write a book
8. Get professional photos taken
9. Give one hundred $100 tips to the beautiful people in the service industry
10. Get a famous person's autograph
11. Play the organ at a Major League Baseball game
12. Attend the Academy Awards
13. Run a 5K race
14. Cook the perfect cheesecake
15. Learn how to say "I love you" in 50 languages
16. Make an announcement over the loud speaker in a grocery store
17. Make a quilt from old jeans
18. Shave my head
19. Ride an elephant in Thailand

20. Get a spray tan
21. Bungee jump
22. Raft down a river
23. Eat a one-pound box of chocolates in one sitting
24. Make a table runner using Hardanger embroidery
25. Add a pottery wheel and kiln to my art studio
26. Make a documentary about suicide
27. Hold a koala in Australia
28. Throw a pencil holder clay pot for each of my kids
29. Eat dinner in Hell's Kitchen
30. Ride a horse on the beach
31. Be an extra in a movie
32. Do a polar plunge
33. Buy a piece of jewelry from every Tiffany store in the world
34. Fight a sumo wrestler in Japan
35. Walk on hot coals
36. Tell the most important people in my life how much I love them
37. Write my personal history
38. Wash all the windows in my house (inside and out)
39. Organize my filing cabinet
40. Serve dinner at a homeless shelter
41. Adopt a cat
42. Paint portraits of my family
43. Weed the flower beds
44. Attend all four Grand Slam tennis tournaments
45. Read a book of scripture from beginning to end
46. Organize my stationery and pens
47. Lose five pounds
48. Give away all my paintings
49. Visit and take a painting class in Italy
50. Crochet a scarf

My 50 Things List:

1. _____
2. _____
3. _____
4. _____
5. _____
6. _____
7. _____
8. _____
9. _____
10. _____
11. _____
12. _____
13. _____
14. _____
15. _____
16. _____
17. _____
18. _____
19. _____
20. _____
21. _____
22. _____
23. _____
24. _____

25.
26.
27.
28.
29.
30.
31.
32.
33.
34.
35.
36.
37.
38.
39.
40.
41.
42.
43.
44.
45.
46.
47.
48.
49.
50.

CHAPTER TWO
What Would I Have Missed?

See the good all around you, even if you have to squint.
— UNKNOWN

I gave myself PERMISSION to kill myself.

BUT ... I decided to WAIT a week,

ONE WEEK—to NOTICE all the things I WOULD HAVE MISSED if had killed myself that day.

These are a few of the things I would have missed:

The words of my daughter: "I couldn't have survived this without you."

The beautiful budding flower in my yard.

The birth of my grandchildren.

The sunset that held so much beauty it couldn't contain itself.

My cat's meow, asking me to pet the top of his head.

Meeting new friends who give me a reason to live.

Feeling the warm sun on my face on a beach in Hawaii.

Eating the perfect watermelon in the summer and the perfect pomegranate in the winter.

Hearing my grandkids tell me they love me.

Enjoying retirement after years of work.

Feeling the utter joy of laughing out loud.*

I have continued doing this exercise every week for the past six years. It has become a habit and still keeps me alive.

*I realized one day that I hadn't laughed for a very long time. I decided I needed to start laughing more and made it a goal. I actually fake laughed until it became real. I found that laughing directly correlated with me feeling less anxiety and stress, and my concerns becoming a little less serious. I felt more happy and emotionally healthy. Laughter truly is the best medicine.

> Put off killing yourself for one week (at least) and write down the things you would have missed if you would have done it today:

CHAPTER THREE

Who Do You Want to Find You?

My worst enemy is my memory.
– UNKNOWN

Someone will find you dead.

That's a fact.

The sight, sound, and smell of a deceased person never leaves.

The person who finds you will never be able to get it out of their mind.

Put yourself in their shoes.

Feel the pain you will cause them.

It will haunt them and negatively affect them forever.

Do you really want to do that to someone?

Killing yourself could possibly relieve YOUR pain but the pain and suffering you create for others will never end for them. Unless, of course, they follow in your footsteps, which will cause horrible pain for others. Unless, of course, they follow in their footsteps, which will cause horrible pain for others. Unless, of course, they follow in their footsteps … you get the point.

Picture an endless line of dominos with your suicide as the first domino. When each one falls it creates horrible, never-ending pain. That your pain will end after death is not guaranteed; but the pain you create for others by committing suicide is guaranteed.

According to the American Foundation for Suicide Prevention (AFSP.org), losing a loved one by suicide not only causes grief; those who witness their loved one's suicide or find the body are likely to experience trauma symptoms. These symptoms include recalling the images of the loved one's body at the time of death, which can prevent one's ability to focus on basic tasks. Other common trauma symptoms include mental confusion and anxiety, and even physical complications such as chest pain, difficulty breathing, digestive problems, and difficulty sleeping. The AFSP also clarifies that although trauma symptoms are most likely to develop for eyewitnesses to suicide, it's not uncommon for any other person to experience trauma symptoms related to a death by suicide.

CHAPTER FOUR

Bad Habit

*We are what we repeatedly do. Excellence,
then, is not an act, but a habit.*
– WILL DURANT

I attended a suicide prevention presentation. At the end of the presentation I asked one question to the presenter. "Why during stressful situations do I automatically turn to killing myself?" Her answer was profound: "It's a bad habit."

I thought about that for a long time and still do. Whenever my mind goes to "kill yourself," I QUICKLY change my thoughts to something positive, such as "go for a walk," "take a deep breath," "leave the situation," "eat a piece of chocolate," "take a nap," "exercise." These replacement responses allow me to break the bad habit of thinking of killing myself as the first and only answer to relieving my stress. I read somewhere that it takes three days to start a habit and three weeks to end one. Give yourself three weeks to end the bad habit.

> **Create a new habit.** Place an elastic band on your wrist and every time the thought of killing yourself pops into your mind, snap the elastic band. Run outside in bare feet until they hurt. Punch your pillow and then scream into it until you have a sore throat. All these things will make you feel alive when you feel most dead.

CHAPTER FIVE

Indecision is Your Friend

Indecision is the key to flexibility.
– FRENCH PROVERB

Deciding on the method of how you are going to kill yourself is your enemy.

Never decide how you will do it.

Make up excuses as to why that's not the way you want to do it.

1. too messy
2. too painful
3. too gruesome
4. might leave you maimed instead of dead
5. might hurt or kill someone else in the process
6. too hard for someone to clean

If you must choose, make the decision to NOT kill yourself.

Once that decision is made, the doors to survival will open up.

Guns = Enemy
Ropes = Enemy
Pills = Enemy
High speeds = Enemy

Avoid them at all costs.

CHAPTER SIX

Go to a Funeral

*There are losses that rearrange the world.
Deaths that change the way you see everything,
grief that tears everything down. Pain that transports
you to an entirely different universe, even while
everyone else thinks nothing has really changed.*
– MEGAN DEVINE

At the height of my depression, a friend of mine chose to kill himself.

He left behind a heartbroken wife and three kids, approximately the same age as mine.

I went to the viewing.

As I looked at the scene—him in the casket, his wife and kids standing next to it with tears and sadness bathing them—I was given a vision.

The person in the casket was me.

I saw my heartbroken husband and children standing next to *my* casket.

It terrified me.

I've never forgotten that sight.

It gave me the strength to live and keep fighting—if not for me, FOR THEM.

CHAPTER SEVEN

Death is Inevitable
(without Your Help)

*This is our big mistake: to think we look forward
to death. Most of death is already gone.
Whatever time has passed is owned by death.*
– SENECA

Death will come to you on its own terms.

It's inevitable for everyone.

No one makes it out of mortality alive.

Don't negotiate with death.

Just wait, it will come.

I'm a procrastinator.

If I can put off:

    dusting

        laundry

            going to the dentist

                taking out the garbage

                    cleaning the toilets

                        or going to the grocery store,

I can certainly put off killing myself.

Be a procrastinator.

Why rush death? It will arrive before you know it, without your help.

CHAPTER EIGHT

How Do You Know the Pain Will End After Killing Yourself?

Pain is a part of life and may also be a part of death.
– UNKNOWN

Ryan Holiday, in *The Daily Stoic*, suggests that there's no guarantee suicide will provide relief from the pains of mortality. He references the thoughts of Marcus [Aurelius, Roman emperor and author of *Meditations*], who believed that manipulating fate's designs could lead to worse consequences and decided to endure his pain the best that he could. Holiday acknowledges the discomforts all of us face and encourages me and you to accept life's hardships with humility, let go of unrealistic expectations of a perfect life, and recognize the power within us to persevere.

> **"Don't fly off to something worse. Bear what you can now. Because you can bear it. We know you can."**
> – RYAN HOLIDAY, *Daily Stoic*

What if the pain and suffering your suicide would create for those left behind somehow transferred to or could be felt by you after you die? Do you want to take the chance of the pain continuing or becoming worse because you killed yourself?

You can master the pain and live through it. I promise, you can.

CHAPTER NINE

Don't You Love Your Friends, Family, and Kids?

The death of a beloved is an amputation.
– MADELEINE L'ENGLE

A therapist once asked me this question: "Don't you love your family?" I answered, "Yes, I do." They said, "Nothing you do in this life will mess them up more than killing yourself. I have been in practice for 25 years and I've never seen anything mess up families more than when a person kills themself." I was hurting so much that the mere thought of putting my family through pain was too much to bear. I decided I would work through my pain so that those I loved wouldn't end up dealing with the negative consequences of my choosing to end it for myself.

> "There is just one way to bring up a child in the way he should go, and that is to travel that way yourself."
> – ABRAHAM LINCOLN

If you kill yourself, who knows how many other people in your life will give themselves permission to do the same.

CHAPTER TEN

Find Something *(Anything!)* to Live For

Do you and I understand that the significance of our service does not depend upon its scale?
— NEAL A. MAXWELL

While I was severely depressed I watched other people giving service to others. Baking bread, making pies, going to lunch, picking up groceries. These seemingly small tasks to others seemed impossible to me when I could barely get out of bed.

I read the above quote and decided something I COULD do was text. I could send out one message a day to someone who was sick or feeling lonely. Later, a woman told me that my texts were what got her through a very difficult trial in her life.

Service does not only count when it's the big stuff. The small stuff counts as service, too.

My dog got ticks. I was the only one who removed them twice a day for a month. It gave me something to live for. This one act literally prolonged my life for one more month. As Temple Grandin said, "The meaning of life is if something that you did made something better," and that's what it became for me. Make it your quest to find someone or something to help every day.

Allow yourself one day to lie in bed, watch TV, wallow in your pain, but decide that the next day you are going to get up and do SOMETHING. ANYTHING. Take a shower. Eat some cereal. Read a book. Take a walk. Send a text. Give yourself permission to have a bad day. Then get up the next day and help someone, even if that someone is yourself. Take care of yourself.

Triggers

There are stressors in everyone's life that send us over the edge. Be aware. Common triggers are: a breakup, an embarrassment, a failure, a disappointment, a chemical imbalance, anniversaries, holidays, stress, pressure, hormonal shit, unmet expectations, fear, marital/relationship problems, social media pressures, etc.

Know your trigger—don't pull the trigger. The cure, remedy, or answer can be as varied as the cause. Find your remedy. Find your way to survive THROUGH the trigger. Service to others is one remedy. Remember, emotions (both positive and negative) are temporary.

Trapped, yet free.

Free to roam, to choose, to fly.

Then why the feeling of being tied up so tightly that I can't move?

That I can't breathe?

Decisions need to be made but I can't muster up enough energy to make them.

Get out of bed? How? Why?

Then a phone call. "I need dinner."

I'm up.

A purpose. I need more than one.

My head hurts. Could it explode? My brain seems to be malfunctioning.

I need a diagnosis.

– JAIME CAPENER

CHAPTER ELEVEN

Don't Believe the Lie

*Once a lie takes root in our minds,
we must drown it out with the truth.*
– JAIME CAPENER

The brain is a fascinating muscle. It can give you feelings of joy, peace, and happiness, but it can also convince you that you aren't worth anything, that you don't deserve to live on this earth anymore, or that everyone would be better off without you.

Oh, how I believed the lies! I knew the truth, but my depression caused me to believe the lies. I finally decided to drown out the lies with truth. I bought a notebook and colored the front cover orange and the back cover blue. When my brain told me a lie, I wrote it down on the pages of the orange side, then immediately turned over the book and wrote down the truth on the pages of the blue side. I did this over and over again until I started to believe the truths.

I used to imagine two people sitting on each of my shoulders. One is rational, the other is irrational. The key to surviving is to ignore the irrational voice and believe the rational one. They are against one another, each one fighting the hardest to win. If you find yourself siding with the irrational side, wait it out. The rational voice will eventually return to tell you the truth. Believe it when it does.

MY LIES AND TRUTHS ARE:

LIE: Everyone would be better off without me.
TRUTH: Everyone would be worse off without me.

LIE: I am too broken to be any good to anyone.
TRUTH: Even in my broken state, I am valuable.

LIE: No one loves me.
TRUTH: Everyone loves me!

LIE: I won't ever be normal.
TRUTH: This might be my new normal, but I am still worth something.

LIE: The pain is too great to live through.
TRUTH: I can live through more than I think I can.

LIE: No one would miss me.
TRUTH: Everyone would be devastated if I weren't here.

LIE: I am good for nothing.
TRUTH: Even my smallest acts of service are needed and appreciated.

LIE: My life is ruined.
TRUTH: I am strong and can survive the trials and changes in life.

CHAPTER TWELVE

Lifelines

Hold a true friend with both your hands.
— NIGERIAN PROVERB

I called my friend to say my final goodbye. She said, "You are serious, aren't you?" Through uncontrollable tears I said "yes." She said, "Listen to me. I need you. I love you. You are my bestie. I can't bear the thought of you not here. Hold on. Sit down. You can get through this. I'm here for you. Just stay on the line. Talk to me." We talked for over an hour until I could face living again.

Another time I called my mom and said, "Mom, I'm ready to do a *Thelma and Louise*. Wanna come?" With a loud laugh, she said, "I'll go fill up the tank!" I was totally serious, but her response surprised me so much that it snapped me out of my suicidal state of mind. We went on to laugh and have a normal conversation. The negative thoughts were replaced with laughter. I could breathe again.

There are times when negative thoughts flood your brain. In those times you forget what is good and positive in your life. Just like my phone conversations with my best friend and mom changed things for me, these ideas can be a wonderful fix:

1. **Make a video with clips of all your favorite things.** Fireworks, your loved one's face, lightning, a stream, your pet, your friend's laugh, the sunset, your favorite flower. Add your favorite music. When you are feeling down, watch the video over and over and over again until the negative thoughts are swallowed up by your favorite things.

2. **Make a compliment catcher.** Get a piece of paper. Whenever anyone says anything nice about you, write those things down on the paper. When you have negative thoughts about your worth, read what is written on your compliment catcher. It will remind you how much you are loved and worthy of living.

3. **Share with others times you felt like killing yourself but didn't.** It will become addicting.

CHAPTER THIRTEEN

Be Rare. Be Unique. Be Weird.

Am I the happiest sad person or the saddest happy person?
– JAIME CAPENER

Be rare. Anyone can kill themselves. Be the one who wants to but doesn't. Own your feelings and live in them. Even at your lowest you are valuable to someone. That's not a lie.

Be unique. Be the one who talks about thoughts of suicide to others. Be the one who gets out of bed even if you don't feel like it. Be the one who calls someone to tell them you are on the edge of the cliff ready to jump, then listen to what they have to say and believe them. Be the willow; it bends but doesn't break.

Be weird. I have always felt as though I was a weird person. I was so severely depressed that I had constant thoughts of killing myself, yet when I desperately searched for the beauty in my life, I also felt joy. I wasn't acting happy to hide my depression; I indeed felt simultaneously happy and depressed. I decided to not give up the joyous times just to get rid of the sad times. I found a way to live through them both, coexisting as it were. That's weird. But I'd rather be weird than dead.

A touch, a hug, a tear,
makes life all too real.
Hard, stone, unfelt
is what I prefer.

My body isn't mine,
my mind isn't either.
Some unknown hell
has taken over.

I want out.
But how?
I want out of my mind and my body.
But please, oh please, let me return when the pain ends.

– JAIME CAPENER

Resources for Help

- 988 suicide hotline
- SpeakingofSuicide.com
- 800-273-TALK (8255)
- Samaritans Helpline: call or text 877-870-4673 (HOPE), available 24/7
- The BlackLine: call or text 800-604-5841
- The Trevor Project, a hotline for LGBTQIA+ youth: 866-488-7386
- Trans Lifeline: 877-565-8860 (US); 877-330-6366 (Canada)
- Copline, staffed by retired police officers: 800-267-5463
- Text hotlines, maintained by the International Association for Suicide Prevention: 741741 (US); 686868 (Canada); 85258 (UK)
- Therapist
- Bio-identical hormones
- Family and friends
- Clergy/Pastor/Priest/Bishop
- OCD/anxiety clinic in your area

Final Thoughts

There is so much love in this world and so many things to live for. You are one of them.

THERE IS A COMMUNITY THAT IS THERE FOR YOU!

This is a living book. In future editions, I'd like to include any tips and tricks you've discovered that have saved your life.

Email me at **50thingslist@gmail.com**

Join me on any social media platform **@50thingslist** and we can build a beautiful community of "us."

ACKNOWLEDGMENTS

This book was very hard to write. While I was going through depression, no one knew the scope of it. I didn't want to burden my family. I didn't try to hide it; I simply didn't talk about it. I was afraid—afraid of so many things. Afraid people wouldn't believe that the happy, outgoing person I was could be depressed. Afraid of being labeled as broken and treated differently. Afraid it would trigger in others the feeling of depression. Afraid people would think I'm only trying to get attention. Afraid people would think I didn't appreciate my wonderful, beautiful life. Afraid of judgement.

Now that the depression has lifted, I look back at it as though it was a different person, a different life. I can talk about it more easily because it is as though I'm not talking about ME. I'm so glad I'm alive to talk about it. You will have the same experience, I promise. Hang in there.

My deep depression lasted approximately 11 years. That's 4,015 days, 96,360 hours, 5,781,600 minutes, and 346,896,000 seconds. So much of that time was emotionally and physically difficult and painful. Yet, I SURVIVED! You can too. The tips and tricks set forth in this book are what saved me. I hope they save you too. You are so valuable.

I'd like to thank my family who suffered through this experience with me. I thank all those who encouraged me to GET THIS BOOK OUT THERE! I express thanks to strangers that I met in restaurant lines who openly shared their feelings and love. I'm grateful to my dear friends who have talked to me about their own struggles and helped me edit the rough, rough drafts. I'm grateful for my editor, Myla Parke, for her work to bring my vision to light.

Lastly, I'd like to thank my God, who walked with me while everyone else was sleeping, held my hand while others were busy with their own lives, stayed with me even when I cursed and cried and whined about how miserable my life was, and quickened my mind and revealed to me many of the ideas included in this book.

AFTERWORD

Often the words, perspectives, and experiences of others can speak life and hope into the darkest of situations. Below is a selection of quotes that have inspired and lifted me. I invite you to mark and memorize your favorite ones, that you might be more empowered to feel and experience the joy that life has to offer you and know that you are never alone on your journey.

"Thinking a smile all the time will keep your face youthful."
– Frank Gelett Burgess

"Anyone can slay a dragon, he told me, but try waking up every morning and loving the world all over again. That's what takes a real hero." – Brian Andreas

"The hardest thing about depression is that it is addictive. It begins to feel uncomfortable not to be depressed. You feel guilty for feeling happy." – Pete Wentz

"One joy scatters a hundred griefs." – Chinese proverb

"Joy runs deeper than despair." – Corrie ten Boom

"When one door of happiness closes, another opens; but often we look so long at the closed door that we do not see the one which has been opened for us." – Helen Keller

"Sometimes the innate strength and hope of a human soul surface only in times of catastrophe or unduly trying circumstances."
– Elaine Cannon

"Don't let what you cannot do interfere with what you can do."
– John Wooden

"Cultivate more joy by arranging your life so that more joy will be likely." – Georgia Witkin

"It appears to me that it is the special province of music to move the heart." – Carl Bach

"Let no one ever come to you without leaving better and happier. Be the living expression of God's kindness; kindness in your face, kindness in your eyes, kindness in your smile." – Mother Teresa

"Let us be grateful to people who make us happy; they are the charming gardeners who make our souls blossom." – Marcel Proust

"Walking, I am listening to a deeper way. Suddenly all my ancestors are behind me. Be still, they say. Watch and listen. You are the result of the love of thousands." – Linda Hogan

"God has infinite attention … to spare for each one of us. … When you pray you are as much alone with Him as if you were the only thing He had ever created. When Christ died, He died for you individually just as much as if you had been the only man [or woman] in the world." – C.S. Lewis

"Start where you are. Use what you have. Do what you can." – Arthur Ashe

"Make yourself necessary to somebody." – Ralph Waldo Emerson

"No one has learned the meaning of living until he has surrendered his ego to the service of his fellow man." – Thomas S. Monson

"Don't seek for everything to happen as you wish it would, but rather wish that everything happens as it actually will—then your life will flow well." – Epictetus

"If you could kick the person responsible for most of your troubles, you wouldn't be able to sit down for six months." – Gordon Gray

"Character cannot be developed in ease and quiet. Only through experience of trial and suffering can the soul be strengthened, ambition inspired, and success achieved." – Helen Keller

"It's the friends you can call up at 4 a.m. that matter."
– Marlene Dietrich

"The only way to get through life is to laugh your way through it. You either have to laugh or cry. I prefer to laugh. Crying gives me a headache." – Marjorie Pay Hinckley

"Make it a point to do something every day that you don't want to do. This is the golden rule for acquiring the habit of doing your duty without pain." – Mark Twain

"What lies behind you and what lies in front of you, pales in comparison to what lies inside of you." – Ralph Waldo Emerson

"Every cloud we see doesn't result in rain." – Quentin L. Cook

"His hero travelled into the past: and there, very properly, found raindrops that would pierce him like bullets and sandwiches that no strength could bite—because, of course, nothing in the past can be altered." – C.S. Lewis

"The best time to plant a tree was 20 years ago. The second-best time is now." – Chinese proverb

"We may feel underused, underwhelmed, and underappreciated, even as we ironically ignore unused opportunities for service which are all about us." – Neal A. Maxwell

"When everything seems to be going against you, remember that the airplane takes off against the wind, not with it." – Henry Ford

"Fall seven times and stand up eight." – Japanese proverb

"There comes a time in life when you have to let go of all the pointless drama and the people who create it and surround yourself with people who make you laugh so hard that you forget the bad and focus solely on the good. After all, life is too short to be anything but happy." – Karl Marx

"When you look past people's imperfections, all that's left are their beautiful parts." – Jaime Capener

"You're safe." – Teal Swan

"What is to give light must endure burning." – Victor Frankl

"Think of the life you have lived until now as over and, as a dead man, see what's left as a bonus and live it according to Nature. Love the hand that fate deals you and play it as your own, for what could be more fitting?" – Marcus Aurelius

"If a man knows not which port he sails, no wind is favorable." – Seneca

"No person has the power to have everything they want, but it is in their power not to want what they don't have, and to cheerfully put to good use what they do have." – Seneca

"First say to yourself what you would be; and then do what you have to do." – Epictetus

"When we are no longer able to change a situation, we are challenged to change ourselves." – Viktor Frankl

NOTES:

ABOUT THE AUTHOR

Jaime Capener is a creator and an artist. She is a friend to all and lets those she meets know that they are loved by her. She is proud to be unique and refuses to mature. The content of this book is from her own experience. She is a reformed perfectionist and survived the ravages of depression for over ten years. She now has a zest for life and is unafraid to talk about her struggles. She desperately wants to help others survive.

www.ingramcontent.com/pod-product-compliance
Lightning Source LLC
Chambersburg PA
CBHW061311040426
42444CB00010B/2593